ALBERTO PINTO
Corporate

Contemporary Offices

Flammarion

Europe and the United States. At that time it was standard practice to deliver completed office buildings bare, devoid of any interior decoration. But Howard P. Ronson had another approach in mind. If all the common spaces were delivered fully fitted out, the effect on potential occupants would be all the more compelling, and leasing more effective. By entrusting the design and furnishing of his own offices to his decorator, Alberto Pinto, Howard P. Ronson was issuing both a challenge and an incentive. The result was conclusive, and Ronson convinced Pinto to take the leap. And that was how, twenty-five years ago, Alberto Pinto entered the corporate world on the ground floor. Ever since, he has been responsible for the common spaces (entrance halls, landings, lifts , private salons, conference facilities, auditoriums, restaurants, cafeterias. . .) in all the buildings built by HRO.

From the outset, Alberto Pinto had to take into consideration an obvious fact: year in year out, countless thousands of people spend innumerable hours in offices. Consequently, it was out of the question to neglect or treat them as indifferent, soulless spaces.

"To my mind, there is no difference between the workplace and living space" he declares with conviction. Throughout his quarter-century collaboration with HRO, Pinto has always maintained his commitment to introducing his trademark charm and grace in all his projects, to exploiting to the utmost the potential of light, scale and volume, traverses and views to the outside, expectations and the unexpected. "One outstanding concept per project."

does absolutely carry his stamp.

A perusal of the projects he has designed and carried out for HRO reveals a number of recurrences; if they don't qualify as obsessions, they are at least pressing demands: the right to eclectism and to ambiguity, the need to combine styles and eras, and lastly, to be willing to go the extra mile for a construction project.

Tradition and modernity, classicism and the contemporary: it would be a gross oversimplification to see Pinto's method in terms of such simple design dichotomies.

Scale, or more precisely breaches in scale, are vital to the designer, who loves to play with the vast and oversized in order to express the monumentality of a space.

His ensembles demonstrate a pronounced taste for noble materials, but he can on occasion use these irreverently to transgress codes in combining, confronting, or even sometimes defying them—with spectacular results. Stone, majestic stone, all types of stone, often predominate in his ensembles. That extra something, the "je ne sais quoi" that sets Pinto apart, is his abiding love of art, ever-present in his design projects: he regularly collaborates with master artisans like glassmakers Bernard Pictet or Guillaume Saalberg, sculptors Jean Faucheur or Stéphane Mocanu, or graphic artists such as Dominique Derive or Florian Schneider.

Pinto tenaciously defends his policy of treating all zones without exception with the same values and codes. Cafeterias, even those relegated to basements, are decorated with bright colors and carefully lit with numerous openings and ample vertical space. Elevator lobbies are glorified by inclining walls or bronze inlays. Linear corridors are metamorphosed into art galleries. Although each of the spaces he treats bears undeniably and irresistibly his stamp, Alberto Pinto prides himself on "never doing the same thing twice." What remains, time after time, is a subtle, refined work on light, tonality, and materials in order to create an impressionistic reading of the space. Nothing could be further from a manifesto; it is the negation of a theoretical discourse, a practical application of a philosophy based on measure, harmony, balance, and elegance. In addition, an interplay of immateriality and compactness, lightness and density manifests itself in a rejection of vain gestures. There is an abiding concern for clarity, form, and efficiency. Each project comes with its specific nature and tells its own story. Each intervention has objectives, a cost, and expresses a culture: opportunities not opportunism, adaptability and otherness. Alberto Pinto's professional credo can be summarized as heeding others, adapting oneself as much to desires as needs, allowing the unpredictable while circumscribing and bringing the inevitable under control. The components are modifiable and transformed from one project to the next, as illustrated in the pages of this book.

HRO Offices
New York City

Left and facing page: The smallest detail is taken into account to assure the passage into the next dimension. Thus, the models of several of HRO's projects, in their materials, scale, and presentation, are more art objects than technical replicas.

Following double page: The anteroom of the HRO offices features thick natural oak paneling, lavender-blue leather chesterfield and matching armchairs, and a stone floor with marble inlays. A series of ceramic panels, treated like traditional Portuguese azulejos, depicts Manhattan buildings by HRO.

Originally, Howard P. Ronson and Alberto Pinto were social acquaintances. They then assumed the roles of client and designer as Alberto Pinto designed house and boat interiors for Howard Ronson. Only later was the decorator persuaded to undertake corporate projects. His maiden venture was to design and fit out Howard Ronson's personal office suite in Carnegie Tower within the heart of Manhattan. Alberto Pinto's gut reaction was to consider it as the logical continuation of his other realizations for his client, a living space rather than a professional one. At least in terms of image, because behind this façade, all the requirements of a contemporary corporate nerve center were meticulously implemented. The result is warm and welcoming, comfortable and elegant.

Madison
New York City

Left and following double page: At the end of the Brazilian rosewood and chrome colonnade stands an endlessly wide reception counter, also in Brazilian rosewood and mirror glass surmounted by an allegorical representation of the five continents by Dominique Derive.

This represented one of HRO's most particularly challenging projects. In midtown Manhattan, in the center of the business district, the complete renovation of an 80,000 square meter office building was masterminded by Skidmore, Owings, and Merrill. The success of the transformation can be measured by the quality of the high-profile tenants that it attracted: JP Morgan Chase, US Sprint, Worldcom, Investment Technology Group, Gulf International Bank, and Varig. Quite clearly, the entrance hall, with its 7.5 meters from floor to ceiling imagined by Alberto Pinto, exerted its influence. This monumental double alignment brings to mind those of classical Egypt at Abu Simbel or Luxor.

Broad Financial Center
New York City

Left and following double page: Italian marbles, Italian and French bronzes, white Alaskan granite: Alberto Pinto has imagined a mineral allegory depicting Wall Street in all its splendor and harshness.

I n lower Manhattan, near the tip of the island, the City groups its vital administrative and financial forces—from City Hall to the Stock Exchange, with nearby Battery Park and the Ferry Terminal. Continuing directly on from Broadway, Whitehall Street enjoys an exceptional topographic location. It was there, along this major artery, that HRO built a 40,000 square meter office building with Skidmore, Owings, and Merrill once again at the architectural stern. Nasdaq, Ernst & Young, Lotus Development Corp., and Telehouse, among others, are tenants. As usual, Howard Ronson called in Alberto Pinto to aggrandize the common areas, which with 12-meter high ceilings have that immoderate potential which is so attractive to the designer's intuitive sense of extravagance.

The excessive proportions are brought under control by Alberto Pinto precisely by exaggerating scale: the 2.5-meter diameter of the clock dial is an eloquent example. As are the 7.5-meter high marble pyramids surmounted by world globes flanking the wall clock. The ensemble creates an impressive blue-tinged atmosphere.

Facing page and right: Alberto Pinto has responded to typical New York orthogonality by generous Latin roundness: consoles, spheres, mirror frames, and inlays all resort to the oval and the ellipse in a clear reference to the Baroque.

Junghof Plaza
Frankfurt

A hundred meters of frontage along the prestigious Junghofstrasse, in the heart of Germany's financial capital of Frankfurt: this exploit, the Junghof Plaza, is a design performance by Skidmore, Owings, and Merrill in partnership with the German architectural firm Nägele, Hoffmann, Tiedemann & Partners.

The stakes were extremely high, because this business center represented a flagship project for international developers HRO. It would be occupied by Morgan Stanley Investment Bank. Alberto Pinto was especially keen to make the building an exemplary display of his work. An added constraint was the fact that Junghof Plaza has two entrance halls that needed to have individual, but nonetheless harmonized, characters. Pinto's idea is simplicity itself, a solution of luminous clarity: the two halls were to be identical, one governed by glass, whereas stone reigned in the second. The highest standard of furnishings and fittings ensures a faultless realization.

Facing page: This is the realm of light. Take for example the extra-white glass slabs carved by the master-glassmaker Bernard Pictet, the large picture windows, and the great glass sculpture by Beverly Pepper.

Facing page and above: Once again, consultation of the preliminary drawings made for this project is edifying in seeing how Alberto Pinto initially envisioned the measure and direction of the design. How can space be expanded? What must be done to allow it to be understood in its most complete dimensions? The response is almost cinematographic in a succession of sequence and tracking shots, dissolves, masterminded through distinctive framing.

For Alberto Pinto, it is unthinkable to consider interior architecture without art being present in some manner or form. It is his approach of bestowing a special spirit on these spaces, that "je ne sais quoi" the French refer to as the soul of a place. Here, art is omnipresent. Just within the doors the glass sculptures by Beverly Pepper and Bernard Pictet are visible. Next, imposing bronze clamps by Stephan Mocanu anchor the reception counter to the floor and lock the wall behind to the ceiling and floor. Bronze cabochons form a grid across the stone walls of the waiting room. The two metal sculptures by Bruno Romeda first attract then focus the glance on the landscaped interior courtyard.

Alberto Pinto always lavishes his attention on reception areas, here leading to the private salons, conference rooms, and the auditorium. Although they are located in a commercial office building, these spaces are, according to his design philosophy, no different from private living rooms. The designer remains true to himself and Junghof Plaza is no exception to this rule which is strictly adhered to. Burgundy stone, Makassarese ebony, Zimbabwean granite, bronze and leather all cohabit in a singularly comfortable atmosphere which is as intimate as it is luxurious.

Left and facing page: The corridors leading to the reception room have been fitted out with the same attentive care. Vast cherry panels framed by Makassarese ebony moldings provide a perfect backdrop for a series of canvases by Kim Rebolhz. Highly elegant furniture by Philippe Hurel graces the salons.

Incomparable comfort, elegance, and intimacy reign in the large conference rooms where walls are covered with light-colored leather panels ornamented with square and circular motifs framed in Makassarese ebony. Furniture by Philippe Hurel and wall lights by Kikko Lopez are integrated into the serene inner sanctum. To prevent, however, any feeling of containment, Albert Pinto very astutely provides opening and depth by hanging a large canvas by Bjorn Wessman.

Above and facing page: Prestige is also the watchword for the 80-seat auditorium where microperforated cherry panels insure perfect acoustics. All decorative elements—large round cabochons, moldings and plinths—are in Makassarese ebony. The deep leather armchairs complete this bronze palette: to quote Charles Baudelaire, "There all is order and beauty/Luxury, peace, and pleasure."

With Alberto Pinto, there was no risk that he would shower any less care and attention on the company restaurant than on the other spaces. At Junghof Plaza, his treatment is exemplary: the walls are lined with maple panels outlined with chrome inlays above a cherry dado. Underfoot, Zimbabwean granite alternates with brown speckled carpeting. Rattan chairs accentuate a warm, carefree spirit. And, so that this space becomes a place of relaxation and reflection, Alberto Pinto transforms it into an art gallery, with a sumptuous series of impeccably framed black-and-white photographs.

Frankfurt is a city with a marked continental climate: hard winters followed by hot summers. The general atmosphere of the restaurant is very cordial; it nestles within a protective and reassuring wood shell. Whenever the weather permits, meals can be taken outside on the smooth concrete terrace that has inlays of French regional stone from Burgundy and Champagne as well as of Zimbabwean granite: in fact it constitutes a contemporary mosaic. Teak furniture converses harmoniously with an extended family of sculptural boxwood topiary.

Arcs de Seine
Paris

This glass monolith, located on the banks of the River Seine, was designed by Skidmore, Owings, and Merrill in collaboration with the French architectural firm, Alexandre and Sandoz. Bouygues Telecom and the French television network TF1 occupy the space. Commissioned to design the interior, Alberto Pinto took complete measure of the vast interior and, drawing his inspira-

tion perhaps from the river nearby, orchestrated an aquatic symphony. With frosted glass, Wengé wood, and white Kashmir granite as principal components, he has composed a décor where light plays an essential role, light in all its translucency, immanence, and unreality. Throughout, luminous glass columns diffuse surprisingly fluid tones, culminating in Venus of the Seine, a sculpture made from slabs of extra-white glass by the very young artist Thomasine Gieseke.

Although Alberto Pinto's design process is often characterized as "instinctive," it can never be emphasized enough that it is actually based on incisive reflection. From the very first roughs to the final result, the concept may evolve, but does not waver from the essential. Alberto Pinto apprehends the whole almost immediately in a quasi-tactile, organic vision, and his equally immediate exactitude allows him to systematize his intuitions and feelings. The proof of the pudding is in the perspective drawings that Alberto Pinto submitted to Howard Ronson months before the first stroke of a hammer: in each, the elements are all in place, accurately and effectively. The sketches are perfect demonstrations that the designer practices the fine art of framing with infinite elegance, transforming the views of common areas into realistic scenes of daily life. These are living spaces to which he adds an additional dimension by introducing art in their midst. Take, for example, this impressive garden of bronze spheres, which Alberto Pinto himself created for the Arcs de Seine.

The science of creating ensembles and an instinctive understanding of materials are essential weapons in Alberto Pinto's design arsenal. In the large entrance hall at Arcs de Seine, he brings together granite, sandblasted glass and Wengé wood in this dialogue of textures and colors. Shadow and light, density and lightness, dark and light confront, answer, and enhance one another. The dialogue continues in the restaurant as ceruse wood and beige carpeting substitute for frosted glass and white Kashmir granite. Wengé wood remains the common link, used for the large vertical waves that structure and divide the space, while the tall Murano glass lampshades punctuate this same space.

H.D. BUTTERCUP

H.D. Buttercup

ALCH CHAIR BLK

H42-1056-791

420129791

Compare at : $300.00

$250

HD Buttercup Price :

L I V E   W E L L

Percentage Off

$ ~~250~~

Was:

$ 195

Now:

ALCH CHAIR BLK

Description:

420129791

Sku No.:

Preceding pages
cafeteria, Alberto
a dance routine v
dear to him: a
kiosks, and stool
to create a fe
ness, though it
controlled. Chro
colorful uphols
relaxation space

Défense Ouest
Paris

This architecture is composed of light eliminate and irreality. Large expanses of transparent glass abolish the difference between the interior and the exterior, increasing accessibility and penetrability. Confronted with this irreality, Alberto Pinto orchestrates a subtle dialectic of appearance and disappearance in the space that he designs. He nonetheless punctuates the evanescence with dark, powerful horizontals and verticals that serve as vanishing lines. Furthermore, to the transparency and translucency, the designer adds abundant mirror play, vertically as well as horizontally, creating a veritable *mise en abyme*. Hence, Alberto Pinto has quite elegantly redefined boundaries, expanded limits, and breathed life into these spaces.

Throughout, the designer calls upon a geometrical vernacular based on the circle, square, rectangle, oval, and the ellipse. It is his manner of introducing an almost imperceptible touch of the baroque within this resolutely contemporary classicism.

Défense Plaza
Paris

Left: A wide sweep of glass of spectacular dimensions opening onto a double-height hall, allowing infinite plays of light.

Standing within the La Défense business district just to the west of Paris, the Défense Plaza is an ambitious office complex, designed by Skidmore, Owings, and Merrill, in partnership with the french architectural firm SRA, combining clear glass, anodized aluminium and natural stone on its façade with elegance and restraint. Taking into account the unique environment that this highly concentrated Parisian business center represents, only services of the highest quality are acceptable. Well versed in delivering the stringent and exacting standards required here, Alberto Pinto has applied himself to the task at hand with his gift for orchestrating infinite variations around a central theme.

Facing page and left: The reception area is a stone symphony. Inlaid blocks of Belgian Vinalmont granite punctuate the highly polished walls made of Jerusalem stone marble. The melange of textures and hues resonates vibrantly.

The walls of the auditorium foyer are clad in Jerusalem stone, enhanced by equally spaced bronze cabochons. Bronze is omnipresent here: consoles, large doors opening onto the auditorium, recessed lights, inlaid floor fillets. Even the four massive floor lamps, designed by Alberto Pinto and crafted in staff by Stephan Mocanu, are in faux bronze. This mineral cosmos is somewhat attenuated by the large lozenges alternated with carpet.

Alberto Pinto pulled out all the stops in his treatment of the auditorium. Above a wrought-oak-paneled dado, the beige flannel wall panels are held together by leather lacing. The leather and oak armchairs are completely adapted to such exclusive sophistication.

Preceding pages, left, and facing page: The concern for detail is a constant preoccupation for Pinto, almost to the point of obsession. A case in point is the subtle leather lacing which links the flannel panels, contrasting the apparently rough copper rings of the lights with the smooth cloth and laces.

Above, left, and facing page: The private salons and conference rooms are located beyond a long, curved fresco by Lenka Beillevert (pp. 62–63). In the conference rooms, the walls are covered with a checkerboard of natural oak panels enhanced by bronze fittings. Mies Van Der Rohe armchairs surround vast oak tables.

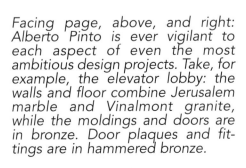

Facing page, above, and right: Alberto Pinto is ever vigilant to each aspect of even the most ambitious design projects. Take, for example, the elevator lobby: the walls and floor combine Jerusalem marble and Vinalmont granite, while the moldings and doors are in bronze. Door plaques and fittings are in hammered bronze.

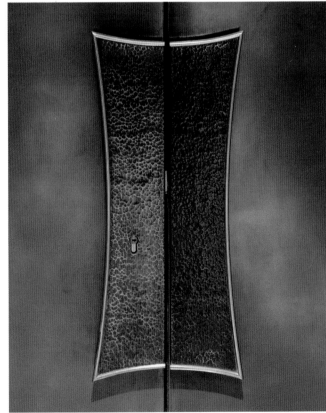

Preceding pages, left, and facing page: In the restaurant, sycamore furniture stands surrounded by wrought oak wall panels, with Forties-inspired plaster wall lights for a period look. But without a doubt, all eyes are on Sheila Hicks's circular textile sculptures.

Europlaza
Paris

A tower in the heart of La Défense needed to be relieved of obvious signs of its ripe age of twenty-five. HRO purchased it and, within the framework of the rehabilitation programs administrated by the local development authority EPAD, transmuted it into a building for the twenty-first century, particularly forceful and with state-of-the-art technology. For this building of more than thirty stories, the building and security codes are particularly stringent.

In this reconversion, the architects Maurice and Frederic Bourstin were allowed to disengage two entire floor levels in order to create an entrance hall that Alberto Pinto has developed into a prestigious portal. Although the space is in itself monumental, the designer has still endeavored to push back the walls and empower its vastness.

Above and following pages: In response to the great expanse of glass along the facade, Pinto has commissioned a monumental sculpture from Jean Reaper. The sculptor has delivered an oversized steel work whose divergent diagonals astutely confront head-on the dominant orthogonality.

Left and facing page: To counter-balance this sequencing, the designer organizes punctuations all along the course, which temper the breaches of scale and serve as stage markers. A metallic orb sits atop a stone pedestal, its image reflecting in the vast mirror behind it, increasing its air of mystery.

n the monumental hall, Pinto disrupts conventions by challenging expectations. Wide expanses of brown granite and beige stone on the walls and floor create depth. Pinto harnesses this vastness and limits somewhat the scale by a festoon of ceiling lights of his design manufactured according to his specifications in the United States. The inspiration for the lights could easily be Art Deco, but could just as easily draw on futurism. The impact is arresting in both cases. A stone and Wengé wood reception console grabs the attention of the visitor, sited as it is in the precise axis of the main entrance.

Facing page: This monumental entrance hall leads to a waiting area of more human dimensions, furnished with deep leather armchairs by Philippe Hurel.

Left and above: A stark and sweeping fresco by Dominique Derive wraps around a massive sculpture.

Facing page, right, and above: Yet another fresco, or rather a freize, envelops the cafeteria, which has white furniture with stainless steel bases. The counters are of solid blackened oak.

Colossal aptly describes the cafeteria, designed to accommodate 950 diners. How to humanize it, bring it within more easily grasped proportions? Through the astute use of color—blue, yellow, green, and pink. Artwork and photographs vary with the seasons. But if there is one masterful idea present here, it resides in conferring a double role to the pillars—both as supports and as gigantic floor lamps. The idea is inspired and sparkles with humor. They only needed to be topped with brightly colored metal lampshades. Not only is there a spirit, but the light suddenly adopts variegated hues. Alberto Pinto also uses chromatics elsewhere to singularize spaces. Of note is the treatment in a very long corridor leading to the private salons (pp. 84–85). There, with an extreme simplicity, he stages a very lively "Gallery of Colors."

Above and right: The framed photographs by Etienne Escoffier lining the cafeteria walls carry the diners to faraway, otherworldly destinations.

Eurosquare I
Paris

Facing page: The beige stone walls and floor are punctuated by dark bands of Wengé wood, while the bronze elevator doors, like vault entrances, add an element of monumentality.

An immense ocean liner has dropped anchor in the midst of the city; a figure-head cleaves the waves. This generously curved structure in an advantageous corner location was designed by the architectural firm, FGDN Architects, to house offices of the French gas company, Gaz de France. Alberto Pinto's response to the evocation of transatlantic luxury ships is to imagine within the vast lobby space a personalized vision which is at once neoclassical and contemporary in its inspiration. This is exactly the transitional style that exemplified the French Line; it was carried out to perfection on their liners *Ile de France* and *Normandie*, where tradition and modernity came together in a perfect decorative fusion.

In the common areas, the repetition of alternating horizontal lines and the choice of materials create a strange, timeless feeling. It is very instructive to consult the preliminary sketches as they illustrate how decisive Alberto Pinto's initial vision of the project was. Once it was commited to paper, the designer remained steadfast to his original idea until the building was completed; the project went ahead unmodified.

Alberto Pinto pays attention to details and especially to expectations. The infinitely polished stone floors act as mirrors, the hammered finish of the metal plaques centered on the elevator doors enhance their stylistic sophistication. The vanishing lines produced by the somber, horizontal wooden bands expand the depth and aggrandize the space. The resulting sense of movement directly evokes the Golden Age of Art Deco. An extraordinarily complex aesthetic is articulated around the line: vanishing lines and convergent points, skillful inserts and inlaid cabochons, accented rhythms and subtle embellishments. This highly articulate design vocabulary reaches its apogee in the bygone heyday of the French ocean liners.

Facing page, above, right, and following double page: Mirror-clad walls extend the circulation space almost infinitely, so that the spatial comfort of both occupants and visitors is preserved.

Facing page and right: The restaurant floor is covered by a carpet of oversized black and red squares. Light-colored oak tables and leather chairs commune with the ceruse oak wall panels and doors. A vast mural by Eric Ciborowski, executed by Stéphane Mocanu, catches then appeases the eye.

Eurosquare II
Paris

In the heart of the new business district in Saint-Ouen, on the outskirts of Paris, L'Atelier du Midi, in collaboration with the American architecural firm Skidmore, Owings, and Merrill, has designed a huge construction of glass, metal, and granite that is occupied by Gaz de France and Nokia.

A foyer of gigantic proportions, encased almost exclusively in glass, provides Alberto Pinto with an exceptional chance to prove his mettle in harnessing natural light. Throughout the entire design process, he also demonstrates his skills of bordering, and especially his taste and understanding of artistic intervention.

Above and right: Underfoot, in answer to and in perfect harmony with the very nature of architecture, polished beige stone is of such perfect smoothness that it seems incorporeal. This immateriality is underlined by equally sleek stainless steel joints.

Left, above, and facing page: These networks of lines and framing remain constant throughout, in space after space. The beige stone and the inlays of fine stainless steel defer, on occasion, to opalescent wall-mounted lights and the bronze elevator doors. Framing accompanies art as it plunges a sculpture by Frode Steinicke into a complex geometrical perspective.

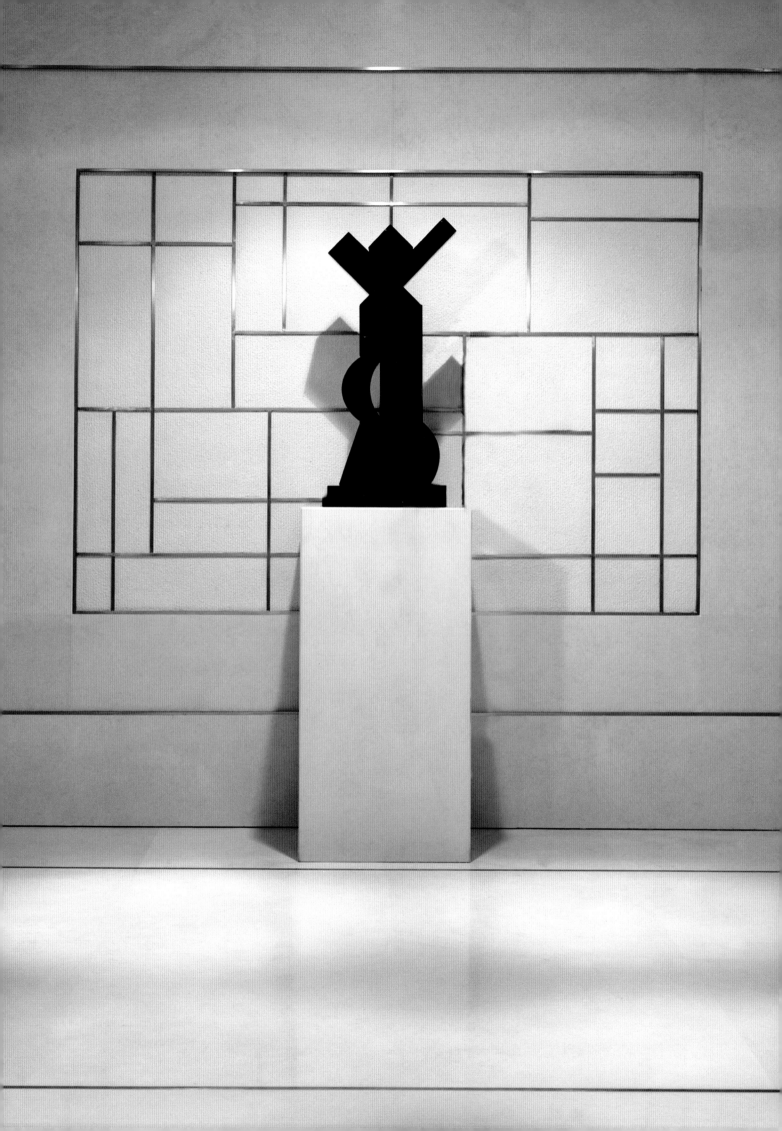

Left and facing page: In the manner of a contemporary art gallery, a dedicated space under the glass canopy houses Venus, a suite of twelve graphic works by Florian Schneider.
Simplified lines and forms structure a very luminous restaurant. Broad panels of sycamore alternate with zebrano on the walls. Underneath, two-tone leather banquettes designed by Alberto Pinto line the walls.

Facing page and right: Comfort is complete in the private salons that open onto the landscaped atrium. Thick rugs atop carpets, deep armchairs and sofas: comfort, tranquillity, and luxury are all important here.

Facing page and above: Beige stone walls, Wengé wood plinths, still more Wengé combined with sycamore for tables, leather seating . . . and on the floor, lines, rhythms, and colors woven into the carpet, designed by Alberto Pinto.

Alberto Pinto has always regarded work spaces with the same consideration as living spaces. Thus, his abiding concern is to humanize them, by giving them a distinctive character. In short, he endows them with a soul. The choice of materials and forms is entirely subservient to this end. Pursuing this same logic even further, Alberto Pinto believes in art in the workplace. Here, a large canvas by Mick Finch hangs near Florian Schneider's *Venuses*.

Left and facing page: Subtle leather lacing runs up and down sycamore paneled walls next to metal lights. On the console stands a strange and primitive sculpture by Stephan Mocanu.

Designed by the Paris-based architectural firm Mas and Roux in collaboration with Skidmore, Owings, and Merrill, Les Portes de la Defense, is incontestably a "high-tech" building. The architects have attempted to foresee and make provision for technological evolutions in order to meet the needs and aspirations of the users. This vision was one that the companies Oracle and Shell both adhered to fully: they now occupy the glass and aluminium edifice. In the midst of

Portes de la Défense
Paris

such state-of-the-art technology, Alberto Pinto has decided to introduce a counterpoise in the form of nature, but not just any nature. Pinto's idea of the natural is diverted and reappropriated. More cultured than cultivated, this forest is petrified, fossilized, reified. A major element of the installation, this forest becomes a leitmotif, which is repeated and reinterpreted throughout. This is yet another occasion on which Alberto Pinto collaborates with contemporary artists.

Facing page: Standing just inside the main door, an immense totem, carved and assembled by Jerome Abel-Seguin, sets the tone. The urban fiber, the din of the metropolis, yield to another world: secure, majestic, and peaceful.

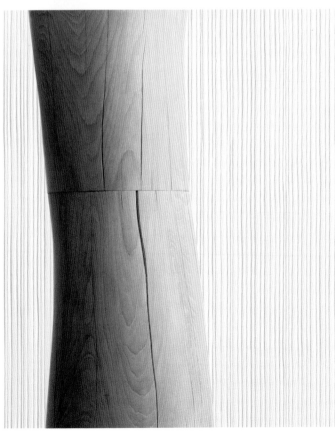

Left, above, and following pages: The three interior halls are interconnected by wood totems and flowers by Abel-Seguin, wrought plaster wall panels by Stephane Mocanu, lights designed by Alberto Pinto, against a background of sandstone and Zimbabwean black granite.

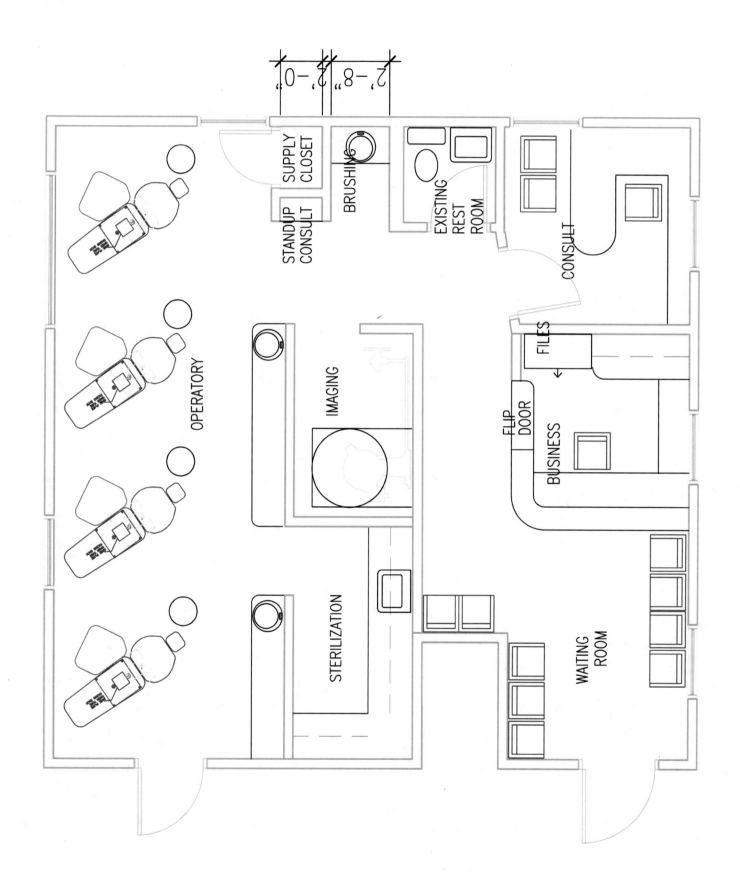

OPERATORY

STANDUP CONSULT

SUPPLY CLOSET

BRUSHING

EXISTING REST ROOM

CONSULT

FILES

FLIP DOOR

BUSINESS

IMAGING

STERILIZATION

WAITING ROOM

2'-0"   2'-2"   2'-8"

Alberto Pinto has an obvious preference for splashes of bright color. While he plays subtly with black and white, his approach to luminous pinks, acid yellows, dark greens, and intense reds is more flamboyant, lavishing them over expanses of walls. Furniture, objects, and artwork become components within chromatic sequences based on intricate rhythms. Here, the floor is awash with an infinite blue that reigns over the space, influencing how all the elements in the decor are perceived.

Facing page and above: A large Balinese palmwood panel orchestrates the transition from the halls toward the conference rooms, leaving behind the forest and moving to smooth, functional tables and consoles by Philippe Hurel.

Above and facing page: To Alberto Pinto's way of thinking, a fitness center requires simplicity and effectiveness, precision and exactitude. Only a stylized panel by Dominique Derive disturbs the dominating abstraction of the gym. The large slats of parquet in the stairwell alternate with special flooring for exercise and sport zones, with the necessary elasticity to add spring to the step. The rigorous alignment of equipment and machines here mirrors the geometrical arrangements of furniture elsewhere in the seating areas.

Facing page, right, and above: Diners at the restaurant find themselves once again surrounded by the petrified forest. Stained strips of bark assembled in collages panel the walls. Underfoot, a gray, mirror-like screed of concrete completes the desert landscape.

Facing page and above: The cafeteria is also within the petrified forest, but in a different, mural interpretation. Here, its effect is softened by the deep blue—almost Klein blue—walls. A suite of small still lifes line the trails.

It is obvious from many of his designs that Pinto imagines his commercial interiors in terms of traffic and circulation. To these ends, he employs colors, furniture, or artwork to direct and emphasize. He is concerned that users and visitors should be able to read a space—or a sequence of spaces—in their fullest dimensions. In much the same manner as a film director, he diversifies his point of view with panoramic or traveling shots, slow-motion, dissolves. . . . As always, Alberto Pinto is encouraging the user to be aware that he is advancing within a sequence and to train his gaze forward.

Left, above, and facing page: It is undoubtedly in the auditorium foyer that Jerome Abel-Seguin's work is at its strangest, acquiring its true artistic dimension. Once within the hand-chiseled wooden doors, a large blue wall is revealed as it is covered by tormented, intersecting lianas from Borneo.

Rive Défense
Paris

An expression of resolutely contemporary architecture, this monolith is steeped in mystery. Another "black box" comes to mind: the famous and equally engmatic one imagined by Stanley Kubrick in his film 2001, *Space Odyssey*.

In response to this rigorous architecture, Alberto Pinto has proposed an interior design program that is at once equally rigorous and contemporary: an arrangement of straight lines structures and gives coherence, expressing the designer's immediate concern for efficiency. The highly luminous entrance hall draws on imagery of futuristic air terminals, while the auditorium is awash with color. The cafeteria is characterized by an emphasis on fluidity, simplicity, and accessibility.

Here once again, Alberto Pinto remains resolute to his initial vision, from the preparatory sketches through to the definitive perspective renderings. Between this stage and the delivered product, there will be no irresolution, no modification.

River Plaza
Paris

Glass, metal, and granite have been combined to breathe life into the outer skin of this 26,000 square-meter building designed by Jean-Jacques Ory and presently occupied by L'Oréal. Alberto Pinto was commissioned to plan and furnish the lobby and reception area, terrace, multifunctional facilities, five private reception rooms, a 500-seat restaurant, as well as a cafeteria seating 100. The result is a very elegant and luminous ensemble with dominant tones of beige stone, white marble, and chrome. Alberto Pinto endorses his realization with his signature horizontal, vertical, and diagonal lines infusing this space with energizing rhythm.

Facing page: Standing directly on the fine beige stone floor, and facing the terrace garden, the black metallic starkness of Stéphane Mocanu's graphic sculpture acts as a sentry.

Bright and flowing, the main lobby maintains its own rhythm, which is united by an essentially graphic vision and accented by regularly spaced lighting radiating from ceiling caissons. With Alberto Pinto there is a constant desire to blur the boundaries between the interior and the exterior. He organizes traverses that encourage the eye to rove, then break loose. Furniture is arranged to create horizontal lines that emphasize the succession of planes and fields.

Facing page and right: Graphics once again, played out this time in the pure, simple lines of beige leather seating furniture contrasting with darkwood slab coffee tables.

Facing page: White marble zigzags animate a long rug of beige stone. By this fluid, almost imperceptible movement, the visitor is visually attracted toward the elevators.

In all of Alberto Pinto's design work there is an abiding desire to create surprise and to avoid the expected. What is quite often overlooked or considered as minor detail become important here, even enhanced. The slanting walls transform the elevator station into a dynamic, intriguing space, accenting its monumental aspects. The sharp turns of the marble bands underfoot are perfect foils to the inclined planes. As for simple wall fittings, Alberto Pinto occasionally practices a little anthromorphism, fond as he is of catching the visitor offguard. Burnished bronze elevator doors give substance to this otherworldly space.

Facing page: The geometrical play of lines continues within the elevators through the association of beige stone and bronze for security and comfort.

Above and left: The five private rooms, which can be used separately or combined, express the same range of comfort and calm.
Works by Dominique Derive lining the walls animate the mood, adding the singular Pinto touch.

Facing page, right, and following pages: White tables and chairs atop chrome bases and legs stand out against the multicolorful explosion of line and form on the walls and floor.

T he restaurant and cafeteria are obvious places for midday breaks, where people are brought together for relaxation and confabs, a place to get away from it all, if only for a short while. To fulfill this role they must be endowed with a specific identity. Complex geometrical effects generated by the repetition of the beveled surfaces of the food counters are intensified by the reflexions of the chrome cladding. Mirrored in the counters are the colorful floor-to-ceiling murals by Dominique Derive that adorn three walls, providing an atmosphere of recreation.

Rives de Bercy
Paris

Facing page: The floor is overlayed by a layer of white Alaskan granite, like a snow-covered vastness of incredible depth. In the axis of the main door, a panel of glass, drawn up and carved by Bernard Pictet, accentuates the surreality of the scene.

André Martin, in collaboration with Skidmore, Owings, and Merrill, has realized an immense edifice of glass, metal, and granite stretching out for more than 115 meters along the banks of the Seine. It now houses the Crédit Foncier de France, a prominent savings and loan association. Although its mass is considerable, it is however much lightened by numerous openings, recesses, and setbacks. The monumental entrance quite naturally opens onto a breathtaking hall. The first impression is one of endless space, immediately followed by one of boundless light. The interior proclaims Alberto Pinto's love of the lofty, which he exploits on every possible occasion. This is evidenced in the overhanging staircases, gangways, balconies, and passageways that enable him to deploy fully his sense of rhythm, movement, and flow.

Facing page and right: In opposition to the immaculate and insubtantial, Pinto proposes density in a subtle exercise that might seem as dialectical as architectural. The great suspended sculpture by Takis and the "Grand confort" sofas by Le Corbusier, Charlotte Perriand and Pierre Jeanneret, exalt black in all its density and depth.

Left, above, and facing page: The restaurant and the cafeteria communicate directly with the Japanese garden. The terrace is a deck of iroko.

sortie

Rives de Paris
Paris

Overlooking the Paris ring road, and facing the student residence halls of Cité Universitaire, the Pfizer Laboratories are housed in an architecture emanating lightness, designed by the Mas and Roux Architects. Alberto Pinto greedily accepts the challenges of this generous space—of vast propositions and dizzyingly high ceilings. Everything is calculated to accentuate the dimensions. Alternating stone and granite, white juxtaposed with black, the decorator repeats half-circles as much as floor ornamentation as to define and enhance the reception area. Artificial light confronts natural light harmoniously, thus adding decorative details in small touches that thicken the plot.

Left, above, and facing page: A massive and yet seemingly floating black Zimbabwean granite reception console dominates the foyer lined with fine, light-colored stone walls. Behind it, oversized sycamore panels are framed by an imposing stained sycamore carved molding by Muquet. To the left, the company masthead is inscribed directly on the stone. Three lampshades which seem to levitate soften the monumental unit.

Left, above, facing page, and following double page: Traditionally, Pinto fits out salons with great refinement. All the components carry on a harmonious dialogue—ceruse oak walls, blackened oak frames, and beige carpet, furniture by Philippe Hurel. The sculpture is from the Pfizer collection.

Preceding pages, above, and right: Throughout the reception and conference rooms, the infinite care that Alberto Pinto dedicates to detail is apparent. Consoles, vases, mirror and photo frames, carpets: all bear witness to this preoccupation. The same attention to detail is evident in the seating furniture by Andrew Worth.

Above, facing page, and pages 152–155: The large black oak table designed by Alberto Pinto constitutes the focal point of the executive conference room. It is perfectly enhanced by a floral triptych and thick, leather-appliquéd curtains.

j'aime la vie
la vie
ne s'arrête
jamais
de marbre et de boue - la vie est
de la vie - la vie d'un sourire -
"assi va la vida" - la vie est comme

Pages 152–155: The seamless procession from room to room is an opportunity to discover works from the Pfizer collection or others especially created for the occasion by Dominique Derive.

Facing page and right: In the restaurant, an immense canvas by Ben from the collection instructs the dining room, a light and airy space of great simplicity marked by white stucco walls and light-colored wooden furniture.

Facing page and above: Darker tones were preferred in the cafeteria where a long counter combines the perfect mix of granite, sycamore, and walnut. Treated in a similar vein, round counters and stools have been placed in a falsely random manner.